eBay Selling Secrets and Tips:

The Ultimate Guide on How to Make Money Online by Selling on eBay

By

Dale Blake

Table of Contents

Introduction 5

Chapter 1. eBay and How it Works 6

Chapter 2. What to Sell 11

Chapter 3. Where to Source Your Items 14

Chapter 4. About Pricing 18

Chapter 5. Tips For Listing Your Items 23

Conclusion 27

Thank You Page 28

eBay Selling Secrets and Tips: The Ultimate Guide on How to Make Money Online by Selling on eBay

By Dale Blake

© Copyright 2015 Dale Blake

Reproduction or translation of any part of this work beyond that permitted by section 107 or 108 of the 1976 United States Copyright Act without permission of the copyright owner is unlawful. Requests for permission or further information should be addressed to the author.

This publication is designed to provide accurate and authoritative information in regard to the subject matter covered. This work is sold with the understanding that the publisher is not engaged in rendering legal, accounting, or other professional services. If legal advice or other expert assistance is required, the services of a competent professional person should be sought.

First Published, 2015

Printed in the United States of America

Introduction

So, by now you've realized that thousands and thousands of people all over the world are cashing in on eBay. Some folks are just selling the odd items lying around the house, others are full time professional sellers and traders. What they all have in common is knowledge and savvy that you lack; knowledge and savvy makes the difference between foundering in the sea of eBay, and riding the wave of sales and trade, high and dry and sitting flush! We'll explore various topics that make an eBay seller a success in this book. These may not all be your style, but by the end you'll have a better understanding of your options, the procedures, the do's and don'ts, and maybe some angles you hadn't considered yet.

Chapter 1. eBay and How it Works

Most people are vaguely familiar with eBay, even if they have never used it personally. We know people sells stuff there. We probably know someone who's bought something there. We might think of it as a widely unregulated free for all full of sharks, and liars, and oddballs selling their garbage. While this concept is not inaccurate, it certainly isn't the whole picture either. eBay has become a substantive global powerhouse, ,rivaled only by Amazon in its volume of trade and global reach. But wild and unregulated? Hardly.

The eBay Community

The eBay community is a disparate and eclectic group of buyers, sellers, weekenders, and first timers. But it is a community with protocol, guidelines, and laws. And to disturb the peace is to be evicted from the community, FOREVER. That's right, if eBay decides to discipline an account holder, that individual is banned for life. They do, in the sense of fairness, have an appeals process, but you'll be hard pressed to find a single story, even on the internet, of an individual regaining their account status once eBay has dropped the gavel. Fortunately the guidelines are pretty straightforward and cannot be broken accidentally.

The first rule of life on eBay (as a seller) is to give accurate descriptions of your wares. That means if there is a small stain on the left lapel of that velour blazer you grabbed at the local thrift shop, you should list it "In like new condition EXCEPT a small stain on left lapel". Then, in your photos, take a picture showing precisely what the stain looks like (more on good photos later). There are two reasons you handle things this way. The first is that bad ratings on your eBay account basically ruin your potential to sell. It's hard enough to sell when you haven't established a good seller rating; it's impossible to sell with a negative rating. Additionally, the buyer has every right under the eBay constitution. If they receive the item and wish to return it for a refund ,they have that right. If they receive the blazer and notice the stain and you weren't completely upfront about it, they're going to be irate. They will want a refund, and still they will hit you with a negative review. This could easily lead to you being ejected from eBay forever and a day. The other reason you want to be honest is that it promotes sales. Most folks that are interested in a velour blazer might be willing to have that item laundered upon receipt, or if it isn't too intrusive, simply live with it. Furthermore, if you are that honest and that straight forward about a little stain, it speaks to your credibility overall as a seller. For the amount of volume that passes through eBay daily, buyers are still extremely wary. Do everything you can to put them at ease, and you'll see your profits climb.

The next rule of eBay is that the buyer is always right. Yep…ALWAYS. They say you didn't do a good job packing the item and it broke in shipping? They're right, you didn't do a good job packing the item and it DID break in shipping. Doesn't matter if you know you triple wrapped it in bubble wrap, two boxes mummy wrapped in packing tape, and that the item you shipped was a river rock…you messed up. They best way to keep your seller rating high is to write-up and save a simple form email that you'll send to each and every disgruntled buyer.

"Dear eBay Buyer,

I am sorry that you are displeased with your purchase. If you will please return the item to sender, I will be glad to issue a full and complete refund. Sorry for the inconvenience"

This is a very power little trick. Many times the buyer will simply drop the complaint as it isn't worth the trouble; they just wanted satisfaction. Also, it helps to foil would-be scoundrels. One common scam is for the buyer to say they are displeased with the product and demand a partial refund. Now, nothing in eBay-land suggests you give partial refunds. Either the buyer purchased the item for the price they paid and they are now the proud owner of that product, or they are displeased, mislead, or otherwise do not wish to own that product, and are therefore entitled to a full refund. It's simple. With this easy email, you can stonewall anyone trying to scam you out of a couple dollars discount. The short story is, maintain decorum at all times.

In the eBay community, your user rating is who you are. If you want to make money trading on eBay, you need to build, foster, grow, and protect your user rating. It's everything to you. In fact, most eBayers, and this goes for hardcore and recreational alike, would rather lose a few dollars here and there to appease a sour buyer, then drop even one-tenth of a point in their user rating. It's that important to your success.

That said, if you are just starting off in the world of eBay, you should focus on building a rating as quickly as possible. To do this, go on eBay and buy stuff. Just buy simple items, everyday stuff, that you need around the home or office. It's not about how much money you spend, it's about the number of successful transactions you have under your name. Once you get your numbers up a little bit (remember buyers are wary) you can get out there and transact your first sales.

Chapter 2. What to Sell

The short answer to this question is "anything you can imagine, and quite a few things you can't imagine". There are lists on the internet of insane items that have sold. It's actually informative to go out and read a few of those lists because it will destroy one of your greatest enemies (in the world of eBay). That enemy? The little voice in your head that says "I can't sell this". That voice is toxic and it must be expunged at the earliest is you want success. If you want to eliminate that voice once and for all, go read those lists of sold items. Then go into eBay's actual listing of completed auctions (under advanced settings) and start to sear random items. 'Roll of Paper Towels', 'Used Baby Bottle', 'One Nike Air Jordan'. You'll soon realize that the possibilities are endless if you're just willing to take the chance to create a market, and you'll also realize that we live in a very, very strange world (but a strange world with a Paypal account!)

Most people get started just selling off the old junk around their home. Clothes are a great place to start, old toys, tools, sports equipment, sports memorabilia, anything with a motif: College, Sports Teams, Disney or

Cartoon characters, Angels, Owls, Frogs, Nostalgia…Old appliances sell well. Realize that what's busted junk to you, is a source of parts or a potential rebuild for someone with different inclinations and talents. Broken electronics are a BIG seller, as are broken tools, and old, worn out, or broken appliances (vacuums are a big hit). We are a nation of tinkerers and dreamers. Your pile of old broken crap could be someone else's fighting robot, or flying drone, or solar powered bicycle.

Think of it this way, for the same energy it would take to gather everything up and haul it to the curb, you could spend that same energy and time listing it on eBay, and actually get paid for it. Now, of course, with most of your junk your profit margins will be too low to interest most people. That's not the point. The point is that with a bit of effort, your garbage will earn you money. With the same amount of effort, you get a greater return on what's not actually garbage. Then if you move up into the desirable items, you can put away some meaning scratch. Many people use eBay sales as a hobby, and buy the time the holidays roll around they have more than enough to do all their shopping. Not into the commercialization of the holidays? Good for you, use it as a vacation fund!

Some items are a more specialty lot. There is money in books, for instance, but they are expensive to ship, and it's easy for the buyer to be unhappy with the condition unless you've actually had it appraised. The same goes for baseball cards, collectors coins, or basically anything where the condition is the main determinant of value. These items are better sold at genre specific craft fairs.

Jewelry and proofs of precious metals however, are a welcome item on eBay, provided you list them the right way (more on that later).

Chapter 3. Where to Source Your Items

We already said, that the best place to get started is right at home. This is the simplest most straightforward way to learn the ropes and get comfortable with the process. You aren't putting out any money yet and you won't be so nervous. Plus you'll be clearing up clutter and it will just come as a pleasant bonus when you actually see the money coming in.

Just real quick about the money thing…some people try to demand checks or money orders, etc. Most people agree, it's a new age, use the technology available to you. It's true, Paypal takes a slice; that's because they offer an insanely convenient service. Now, if the buyer is coming to your home, obviously suggest a cash transaction, but otherwise just bite the bullet, render unto Paypal and make up the difference by pushing higher priced items or increasing sales volume.

Ok, so you've picked some items from around the house, you've opened your eBay account (simple and step-by-step) and you've made a sale. Now, it's safe to assume, you've laid in bed just imagining the possibilities of what you can do. You've been bitten, like so many others. No use trying to deny it. Take that energy and roll with it.

Do you want to finally turn your crafting or carving hobby into an online business? Start on eBay. Want to clean out your entire house and post it all? Your returns will be many times higher than they would be from a yard sale. But maybe your mind has turned in a little more businesslike direction. Perhaps you thought of your neighbor's garage sale last Saturday. They had some neat stuff didn't they...and cheap. That old art-deco lamp they were selling for $3.00 just to be rid of the darn thing...didn't they have a box of original Sega games too? They were $0.50 each, and you remember reading an article that mentioned they will often sell for $5-$15 on eBay, out of box, condition unknown. Oh my goodness, you could have made one hundred, maybe even two hundred dollars from your neighbor's garage sale alone. There were 15 garage sales in the area that weekend...$100X15= One heck of an opportunity.

Now, maybe you're wondering now, well if it's so easy and profitable, then how come everyone isn't doing it?" And I say to you..."you're not doing it are you smarty-pants". People just don't believe that they can successfully make money on eBay and they are just wrong. They are afraid to start, think it's more complicated than it is, or believe there's risk involved than there actually is. Now garage sales have maybe the highest profit margin per item. For the weekender or the hobbyist, they are a great way to earn some extra cash, get outside, and feel pretty clever at the same time. But some people want to get more serious about it.

One way to create yourself a side business is to sell a regional specialty to a national (or global) Market. If you live up on the coast of main, package up some of these beautiful speckled beach rocks. Cost to you - $0.00 price on eBay $10-$20. Live in New Mexico, you can do the same with Rose Quartz. Pennsylvania has all the handcrafts made by the PA Dutch and the Mennonites, maybe you live near a Native American population or a First Nation people...Maybe you live in New York City. Do you have any idea how hot I-heart-NY shirts, hats, etc. are on a global market?

Want to go one step further? Become an importer...no, seriously. What some people are doing is combining the power of Alibaba and eBay (or Amazon). They go on eBay and search which items sell well consistently over time. You want something that is not novelty driven (no cell phones) and an item whose obsolescence is a still far off (no tape recorders). Something like kitchen gadgets, hand-held scanners, or tool sets meet these criteria.

Next, you go on Alibaba and search for manufacturers and distributors of the product you have chosen. Contact each of them and ask for a price quote, shipping included, for 5 -10 -50 -100 of that item. Collect all your quotes and find the best offer. Remember, you have to consider both the cost-per-item, and the overall shipping rate. Once you have your choice, order 5 or so of the product to test that shipping is efficient, and that the product meets your standards. You can then go ahead and list that product at an appropriate price point, and thus begins your own import business...amazing.

Chapter 4. About Pricing

How you price your items, and the manner of sale you choose are extremely important, and often overlooked parts of the eBay process. There are few theories, but if you take a survey of successful eBayers they consistently agree on most points. This is because eBay has a rhythm and consistent that you, as a savvy seller, can capitalize on.

The first consideration is to go with the auction style, or buy now. These features both have their place in eBay sales, but they are not mutually interchangeable. One must consider the mentality of the buyer when deciding how to list your items. Is it a hot commodity, a common good, or a unique item with a limited market? Will you have much competition in trying to sell your item? How long can you wait to make the sale?

Buy Now

Let's begin with the 'buy now' option for eBay sales. Many sellers use this option exclusively. They feel that it allows them a reliable profit on items they sell. These sellers tend to sell the same items over and over again (Ralph Lauren polo Shirts, Kitchenaid stand mixers, etc). They enjoy the consistency of knowing what they will earn, and once they have found a price point that works for them, they simply let the flow take over and manage their accounting from the point of view that sales will more or less be consistent.

The drawbacks to this approach are twofold. First, there is always the chance (certainty) that someone else will come through with the same strategy and undercut you. This actually takes on the dynamics of a traditional retail setting, where a pricing war takes place and eventually one of the competitors folds leaving the entire market share to whomever can keep prices low and costs lower.

The other big drawback to the mentality is that it misses the opportunity for bidding wars. Now, with a generic item, you will not generate much buyer enthusiasm, and therefore can't expect much from an auction. In fact, with lackluster items, due to the manner in which you price auction items, the seller would frequently sell at minimal profit . If you are selling something that's a dime-a-dozen, then maybe that's exactly how you should price it…at a flat rate.

The other time that 'buy now' listing is your best bet is when you are selling to an extremely niche buyer. Let's say you have two sets of wiper-blade arms for a 1968 Datsun. In that case (do your research first) you may not be looking at a large pool of buyers, but rather a unique group of people that will absolutely buy the item if that's what they're looking for. In this scenario, you are in the driver's seat (sorry for the pun) and you can set your sale price much higher. Then you just sit back and wait for that particular buyer (that buyer is out there somewhere) to come along and accept the offer.

What many savvy sellers do is to take a unique item like that and post it for auction once or twice before putting it up for the 'buy now' option. They set the initial price pretty high, like 10% below what they really want for the item. If it doesn't generate interest, then you know you've got a sleeper and it's best just to sit on it and wait for the right buyer to come along.

Auction Selling

For many people, especially buyers, this is the most fun and exciting part of eBay commerce. If you are selling random items that have a market, and most items have a market, then auction is definitely the model you want to pursue. It allows you the chance to generate competitive bidding, get some real enthusiasm going, and ultimately to capitalize on people's competitive nature.

One sensitive point on auction sales is where you set your starting price. Too high, and you won't generate the type of interest you want. Too low, and you risk losing money on a sale if it was just a slow period (those do come and pass). A good safe starting price requires you to be honest with yourself. "What is the minimum I will be happy accepting for this item". It's not about what you want to make, it's basically a tiny fraction above your break-even point. Now, there's some flexibility here. If you found a nifty mirror at a yard sale and you paid $5.00 for it, and you're certain it's worth $20, and you'd like to get $40-$50, then set your start point at twenty dollars. With a little experience you'll learn to predict the probable increase in an auction sale from start price to sale price.

Another way to gain an idea of where items sell is to go to the completed auctions page. Auctions in red never successfully finished in a sale. The rest will show you what the market is willing to pay for various items. You can use this information as a rough guide to setting your own base prices, but don't get carried away. Remember, the key to a successful auction is to have as many interested parties as possible engaged in the bidding. Even if, in the end, there are only two or three parties truly interested in obtaining your item, the early comers will organically drive up the sale point, all to your benefit.

Chapter 5. Tips For Listing Your Items

There are some things you can do to stand out in the crowd. The first, as we discussed earlier, is to always increase your user rating. Do anything you can to make sure it climbs and climbs again. Long time eBay buyers will instinctively glance at that rating and simply pass over someone who hasn't made a mark in the game. That doesn't mean you won't make ales in the beginning, but it means that as your user rating increases, so does the pool of serious buyers that are giving your listing their full attention.

Next, give thorough and honest product descriptions. This entices the buyer's interest and makes you seem more thorough and trustworthy. Also, use keywords in your descriptions. List brands, labels, years of production, logos, teams etc., and colors and sizes. eBay works on a key-word search principle. The more unique identifiers in your product description, the better the odds are that motivated buyer will come across your listing.

Finally, a few words about photos. There's advice out there telling you to use stock photos, or copy photos from other people's completed auctions. This might work fine if it's "Fruit of the Loom Men's XXL White Cotton T-Shirts, New in Original Package" because everyone knows what that looks like. We don't need an artistic rendering of a cross-lit package in low lighting…just the facts will do here.

When your item is more unique, your photographs will generate interest better than anything else. Take pictures from multiple descriptive angles. Take some time to look at the photographs other people take until you start to develop an understanding of the difference between a picture and a descriptive picture. Shoot from multiple angles if your item has more than one side. Shoot it from far off. If there are any flaws, blemishes, stains, cracks, etc. take a close-up photo of that spot and a distance shot indicating its location on the item. Include some size reference in these photographs. A ruler, or coin will work well to communicate how significant the flaw really is. Many buyers will overlook an item in less-than-perfect condition if they have a good sense of what they're getting.

If you are selling an item that is valued by weight: gold or silver proofs, precious and semi-precious metals or jewelry of the same, then weigh it on a small precise scale. Include a photo of the item on the scale where the buyer can clearly see the readout. Likewise, if you are selling some type of electronic device, and it is in working condition, take a picture of it turned on and working. In short, use for photographs to give the buyer information so that you don't have to ask them to 'trust you'.

The world of selling on eBay can be fun, interesting, exciting, and profitable. Take your time to learn the ropes while you're getting started. Begin with one item and see how it goes. Likely, you'll be surprised how easy it can be to sell things from around your home; items that would have gone for $5 at a local yard sale can easily grab you fifty or more if you happen to hit a hot streak . Always think in the terms of your buyer when listing, pricing, photographing, packing, and shipping your items, because this will lead you to profitable decisions. If you are going to make a business of it, even a side business, remember that volume generally produces the best returns. However, don't be shy to be aggressive with something special.

You'll quickly begin to spot items at yard sales, estate sales, thrift stores, and even at the homes of your friends and relatives. You'll develop eBay-dar and you could easily find yourself at swap-meets, auctions, yard sales, and goodwill at times when otherwise you would have been sitting at home.

Conclusion

Times are changing and the ones able to get in early are going to benefit the most. With a bit of pluck, some creative thinking, basic computer skills, and the courage to ignore your own unfounded doubts, you too can be buying low and selling high. You'll love the feeling you get when you turn that junk and clutter into real honest income. Who doesn't want less mess and more money? Go on and get started, there's a whole world of opportunity collecting dust right in your own closet.

Thank You Page

I want to personally thank you for reading my book. I hope you found information in this book useful and I would be very grateful if you could leave your honest review about this book. I certainly want to thank you in advance for doing this.

If you have the time, you can check my other books too.

www.ingramcontent.com/pod-product-compliance
Lightning Source LLC
LaVergne TN
LVHW021748060526
838200LV00052B/3550